MEMORIES

— in —

DRAGONFLIES

MEMORIES

— in —

DRAGONFLIES

Simple Lessons for Mindful Dying

LANNETTE CORNELL BLOOM

SHE WRITES PRESS

Published August 21, 2018
Printed in the United States of America
Print ISBN: 978-1-63152-469-1
E-ISBN: 978-1-63152-470-7
Library of Congress Control Number: 2018934193

For information, address:
She Writes Press
1563 Solano Ave #546
Berkeley, CA 94707

Interior design by Tabitha Lahr

She Writes Press is a division of SparkPoint Studio, LLC.

Names and identifying characteristics have been changed to protect the privacy of certain individuals.

For Mom, for so much.

Note to My Readers

*T*his book started on the tail end of a dream. I awoke one night, years after my mom had passed, with the inexplicable urge to write down my experience of taking care of her. I no longer felt the fresh grief of losing her, and I definitely did not consider myself a writer. Yet all of the memories were there, just waiting to move through me and into the world. The next morning I bought a spiral notebook and started what would become three hundred pages of handwritten memories by the end of six months.

I could not believe the extent of the details that I remembered about such a hard and tragic time in my life—a time when I kept my head down, suppressed my grief, and took care of things. But as I dug deeper and deeper into those moments, the truth was I could not recall the sadness. What I did recall was a blossoming awareness, an awakening to the simple joys that lurked beneath the surface of hardship.

While the following pages recount the journey I took with my mom, I want to say up front that whatever your reaction to your loved one's passing, you are doing it right. There is no one way to move through this process.

This book was not intended to be an exploration of grief, a how-to guide for taking care of a loved one, or even strictly a memoir. As I wrote and rewrote, remembered and recalled, this book's purpose became clear: to inspire.

My hope is that this book may open you up to the more magical side of death. That even within the darkest times of your life, you may find hidden some connection, healing, or—dare I say it?—sacred joy.

Contents

Chapter 1: The Diagnosis

*I*t started with a cough that would not go away—a light, dry cough, almost like a tickle in the throat. But with each passing month, my mom's cough persisted, stronger and louder. In the air conditioning at dinner, the cough shook her frame. At night, the cough woke her mid-dream. In the midst of a conversation, the cough stopped her words short.

She saw doctors. They ran test after test. A gastroenterologist ordered her to eliminate alcohol, then acidic foods. A pulmonologist treated her for pneumonia. But the cough remained. Finally, after a year and a half, at age sixty-three, my mom went to see a specialist that my dad had insisted she *please, give a chance.*

This specialist ordered another MRI and CT scan, and we were hopeful that this was it—that we would finally get a concrete answer, and a concrete treatment.

A few weeks later, as the last bell rang at the high school where I was a nurse, so did my phone. The caller ID read: Dad. As I opened the flip phone, a group of sophomore football players dragged a half-conscious boy through my door.

"I have to call you back," I muttered into the phone and slapped it shut.

"He passed out on the field!" one of the boys said.

I helped the lethargic boy into a chair and examined him, asking the others questions. Did he hit his head? Was he drinking water? Did he normally slur his words?

By the time I assessed him, treated him for low blood sugar, and waited for his mom to get him, it was nearly evening. I rushed home to find my teenage girls doing homework on the couch, my husband not yet home from work, and no dinner on the table. I peeled the cluster of Post-it notes off the inside of my purse and began to sort through them:

Pick up dry cleaning and *make dentist appointment* into one pile—not priority.

Buy laundry detergent, birthday card for Sis, and *brownie ingredients* into another pile—pressing, yet forgotten to-dos.

I rubbed my forehead. A sticky note fell from my jacket. I read it upside-down: call Dad back.

I peeled it off the ground and pressed it onto the counter in its own pile—I'd call him after dinner.

As I pulled spaghetti ingredients out of the pantry, my phone rang again. Dad.

I flipped the phone open. "Hi, sorry, it's been a crazy day. Can I call you after I make dinner?"

Dad cleared his throat and his voice came out steady. "Your mom and I just need to talk to you about what her doctor said. Can you come over tomorrow at ten?"

"Of course," I said, setting down the cans of tomato sauce in my arms.

"See you then," he said, and the line clicked.

What did he not want to say over the phone?

I called my district office and requested the day off from work—something I never did—and the next morning drove out to my parents' house.

I waited at their front door as my sister parked behind my car and then walked up the long driveway to meet me. Though in appearance our four-year difference seemed to shrink with time—our blonde hair was evening out to the same short length, our small frames were filling out to our family's genetic "country stock" build—in our relationship, something always seemed to separate us. Growing up, we managed to just miss each other before moving on to the next level of schooling. When I got married, she was finishing school. When she got married, I already had children. Now, our children—mine girls, hers boys—had a decade between them, and it seemed to put that much more distance between us. We lived in the same city, but it was Mom who made sure we maintained a connection.

When we entered the house, Mom and Dad were sitting at the dining room table. The ticking grandfather clock magnified the otherwise silent room as we sat down. My parents' intentionally blank expressions failed to hide the pain behind their eyes as Dad took Mom's manicured hand in his rough, wrinkled one.

His years of working outdoors as a large animal veterinarian were catching up to him; his black hair had faded to white and his fair skin was now wrinkled and covered in sunspots. His six-foot frame was a few inches less, with back pain stemming from his golden days as a bull-riding cowboy. Despite age weighing him down, to me Dad was still a strong, commanding presence. But as he opened his mouth, he suddenly seemed frail, lost. His voice wavered as he told us, "Your mother has been diagnosed with pulmonary fibrosis."

My breath left me.

As a nurse, I knew what this diagnosis meant. Mom's lung tissue was scarring, becoming solid. In time, air would no longer move in or out of her lungs. In time, she would suffocate. I was about to witness the person I loved most fighting for each breath.

I looked away, to the timeworn record player behind them, to the still life painting hanging on the wall, to the American Indian wooden kachina dolls lined along the display table connecting the dining room and living room—their silly, blank expressions staring back at me. All of them shrank with irrelevance.

I clenched my fists under the table, the fire in my gut fighting the ache in my heart. After all the doctors, all the tests. We had wasted so much time and now . . . we would be lucky if Mom lived a few more years.

It made no sense. Mom was nothing if not two things: health-conscious and happy-conscious. Her motto was, "think happy thoughts," and though we marveled at how she was able to do it, she always seemed to find the best in every situation. She read Hallmark cards as often as *Reader's Digest*, and shared inspirational quotes as often as she preached health and nutritional advice. How could someone who took such good care of her body and mind be terminally ill?

I looked back to Mom, and she smiled over at me with solemn courage.

It was smaller than her usual smile—the smile that could light up the room, the smile that often transformed into her signature laugh, a polite giggle that could only be described as delightful.

The fire in my gut lessened. I knew I never wanted her to lose that smile.

What I did not know—what I could not know—was that even though we would fight to maintain a semblance of life as we had always known it, we were about to embark on a spiritual journey that would change us all.

Chapter 2: Build Your Bridge

Four Years Later: August

The metal flag on my parents' mailbox whined as I yanked it back into the down position. The stack of mail was larger than usual, and on top was a white envelope with the blaring red words, "FOURTH NOTICE."

I had been driving out to my parents' house a couple times a week since Mom's diagnosis. I had made the difficult decision to quit my job as a school nurse to be there for her. Still, my list of to-dos seemed to keep growing, now that it was combined with my parents'. I was running on empty moving between two households, and it felt like I was trying to keep a lid on two pots that always seemed to want to boil over. Retrieving the mail had become one of the to-dos when I visited my parents' house. With a bag of dirty laundry over one shoulder and a bag of groceries on the other, I tucked the pile of mail under my arm and walked up to the house.

"Dad, it happened again," I called.

He wandered in from the living room and I handed him the threatening tax bill.

Dad's brows crinkled. "Another notice? Your mother swears she paid it."

Mom had done all their bookkeeping, both business and personal, for as long as I could remember. She had never forgotten to pay a bill. Ever.

"I'll look into it," I said, and began separating the rest of the mail.

Dad let out a heavy sigh and slid another letter over to me. It was from the local department store. But it was not a department store bill—it was the tax check signed by Mom.

For months now, we had been ignoring the undeniable—that Mom was becoming forgetful, that her appetite was lessening, that she could no longer lift her two-pound exercise dumbbells. Over the past few years, the doctors had been steadily increasing her medication to fight the progression of the disease, but it was now clear that the side effects were beginning to take over her life.

The murmur of a car engine stole my attention and I glanced out the window. Mom's blue Jaguar rolled into the driveway, the front grill dented.

My heart leapt. I looked to Dad, whose eyes were wide. We rushed to the front door.

Mom walked slowly up the pathway, her face paler than usual, the car keys dangling from her shaking fingers. "I don't want to drive anymore," she said.

We sat her down at the dining room table, and she confessed that when she had pulled in to fill her car up with gas, she had accelerated instead of braking, driving directly into the yellow pole that blockaded the gas pump.

My mind raced with images of flying metal and fiery explosions.

"I don't want to drive anymore," Mom said again, her voice cracking.

A familiar tightening built in my chest. Mom's distressed face filled my vision. A sense of resolve stirred within me, instilled in my bones when I was a little girl.

When I was three years old, my parents and I lived in a twenty-eight-foot trailer across the street from Dad's veterinary school. Mom was twenty-three and pregnant with my sister. Dad was twenty-four, working odd jobs in animal care around his school schedule so we could all scrape by.

Mom and Dad were on the couch with our boxer puppy, Coco, and I was feeling restless. Like most kids my age, I started twirling to entertain myself.

"Should we stop her?" Mom asked.

Dad must have answered "no," because, for the first time ever, neither of them stopped me. Round and round I went like a spinning top until the dizziness took over. I teetered sideways, my head catching the corner of our coffee table.

Pain shot through my temple. I let out a wail of anguish as something hot and warm trickled down my cheek. My chest began to tighten, panicked breaths fluttering out of me with my tears.

Dad scooped me up and held a cloth to my head, applying pressure to the gash. "There's surgical tape in my bag," he said in a calm voice to Mom.

My wound continued to throb, growing more painful with every second.

"She might need stitches," Mom said in an anxious tone, walking to the opposite end of the trailer and rummaging in Dad's bag.

"She'll be okay," Dad said as he blotted my forehead, took the surgical tape from Mom, and stuck it across the cut. Then he said the words I would never forget.

"You're a Cornell. You can take it." He kissed my forehead.

My heartbeat slowed as my focus narrowed to Dad's calm face.

I nodded, suddenly feeling just as calm, despite the incessant ache.

Though at the time I could not have known, our family did not have health insurance. A trip to the emergency room would have put my parents in debt.

That day I learned the resolve that was deep in my parents' hearts. We took care of each other. We stayed strong when facing a problem until we figured out how to solve it—even if we wavered in the moment.

I reached across the table and took Mom's hand. "I can drive you," I said. "I'm here."

She squeezed my hand back.

Neither of us let go.

And in that moment, I knew that this was the true start to our journey, that together we had just stepped onto a bridge. And though we could not see what lay in store at the end, what we could see were our entwined hands, holding on tight.

Chapter 3: Take a Deep Breath

September

*M*om looked up to see Dad pulling a large box into the kitchen. Her face tensed in recognition of what was inside. Not because she did not want the oxygen, but because it meant dragging around a tank connected by tubing to her nose.

Thanks to her regimented beauty routine each morning and night, Mom had managed to keep up her appearance. She looked herself. Her blonde hair was flipped under perfectly. Her crystal blue eyes remained bright. Her complexion was as soft and creamy as ever, with very few wrinkles lining her face. And—to her delight—her thin build was slightly thinner. Aside from the relentless coughing, which she quelled as best she could with cashmere scarves and cough drops, she did not appear to be ill.

When Mom did have to cough in public, the first words out of her mouth were, "I'm not contagious." She had always been hyperaware of how she moved through the

world, which made the undeniable truth even harsher—
Mom needed help breathing.

I sat with Mom at the kitchen counter, on her favorite
wooden stools lined with soft, beige leather. Her oximeter, which measured her blood oxygen level, balanced on
her right index finger. She waited patiently for it to reveal
its magic number, answering the question: would she be
within the normal range? It was becoming an obsession.

My cell phone buzzed for the third time that morning.
First my daughter, then the pharmacy, now . . . the same
caller ID that had lit up yesterday: the district office for my
old school nursing job. I had already listened to their first
message—would I consider working as a sub? After I had
declined their offer to come back full-time, this was what
they considered a good compromise. My head pounded
with the pressure of the decision.

The numbers on Mom's oximeter blinked. Lower than
last time. Below normal range.

My phone gave a final, desperate buzz, indicating
another voicemail. Not long ago, I would have agreed
that the district office's offer was a good compromise. But
I could no longer fulfill their needs on top of everything
else. Managing Mom's health—keeping her infection-free,
monitoring her medication, her diet—was our biggest
weapon in this fight against the progressive scarring in her
lungs. And it needed close to my full attention.

Dad ripped the tape off the top of the box and
unpacked all the oxygen equipment. Mom's jaw lowered
further with each piece—the huge tank, the wheeled pulley,
the tangled tubing.

"The tank is so big," she said. "How am I going to pull
that around?"

"Don't worry," Dad said as he pushed the box aside.
"We'll get this all organized."

She nodded, though she could not contain her anxiety. "I was hoping it would not be for a long, long time." Light tears streamed down her cheeks.

I fought my constricting chest as I pulled her close.

"This is how I have to live?" Her voice quavered.

I hugged her tighter. "It'll be okay, Mom."

Dad stood and disappeared down the hall toward their guest bedroom.

He and I had anticipated that Mom would react this way. The book of rules she had lived by her entire life—the rules she'd enforced while I grew up—were slowly being undermined by her illness. The rules dictated how to be a proper family, a proper lady, and how live a proper life. Being sick—*looking* sick—was against the rules. And while Dad and I wished she'd throw the rules out the window, we understood she might need to cling to them even more now, to maintain a sense of normalcy.

I noticed in that moment that I was becoming less a participant in these rules and more of an observer. There was no way to do any of this perfectly, by the book.

A few minutes later, he returned and placed a pair of glasses on the counter. "I did some research online," he said. "These will hide the tubes."

Mom picked up the eyeglasses. The design allowed the oxygen cannula to run through the earpiece and along the nosepiece. The lenses themselves had no prescription—exactly what she needed.

Dad attached the tubing to the glasses and gently placed them on her face. "No one will notice what they're really for."

Mom smiled.

And my heart buoyed.

Anything for that smile.

Chapter 4: Ignore the Clock

October

"*I* want you to go," Mom said one fall afternoon, just a week before I was set to leave on a sixteen-day Arts and Crafts bus tour that traveled through the northern part of India, a trip I'd committed to take with my husband and mother-in-law months earlier. "It's a special opportunity, and I won't be the reason you don't go."

Her words came out in short, deliberate spurts. I nodded, staring not at her, but at the tubing that ran into the den, to the oxygen machine. Its low drone interrupted the silence.

She was right. It was a-once-in-a-lifetime opportunity. While in India, we would stay in various palaces and forts and learn about the culture—the food, the history, the art. My husband was really looking forward to our going, and we were both looking forward to the quality time it would afford.

Yet, just a month earlier, Mom had started using the oxygen tank. *How could I go on this trip when these might be my last moments with her?*

Mom cleared her throat. When I looked back at her, a silk drawstring pouch rested in her palm. She offered it to me. "Give yourself this break."

I loosened the drawstring and out slid a brilliant round crystal, wrapped in a folded note written in her handwriting: *For safe travel. This is a path maker crystal.*

"I take this with me every time I travel," Mom said.

"You do?" My brows knit together as I examined the crystal. It was beautiful; its many facets glimmered in the lamp light of the den. *But did Mom really believe it would protect me?* Not to mention, I would be more concerned for her well-being than my own while I was gone. *But still, if it would make her feel better . . .*

I replaced the crystal in its pouch and set it in my purse. "Thank you, Mom. I'll take it with me."

A week later, I was on a plane, and then on a bus in India. Our driver was navigating the narrow streets, while the co-driver defended our slice of road. He shouted injustices at bicyclists weaving in and out of the traffic, cows grazing, and men barbecuing in the middle of the street. Smoke and the smell of curry seeped through the cracks of our bus's windows—an aroma I began to associate with breakfast, lunch, and dinner.

I tried to immerse myself in my surroundings, focusing on the beauty amidst the chaos. I was drawn to the women adorned in colorful saris that draped delicately to the ground and made the women appear to float like clouds as they walked. I marveled at how all the shopkeepers swept their dirt floors with brooms—homemade of stick and straw—so thoroughly that the dirt compacted into a smooth surface, almost like concrete. And yet, anxiousness sank its claws deep and would not let go.

Halfway through the trip, after a long distance call to Mom and Dad, my fears about leaving home were validated. Mom's new MRI results showed that the scarring in her lungs had progressed.

"I'm coming home," I had said emphatically over the phone. I wanted nothing more than to leave my room and hop in a cab to New Delhi's Airport three hours away. I would sit in the airport for as long as it took to get on a flight home.

"No," Mom said. "You're almost done with the trip. Finish it and learn what you're supposed to learn. I'm okay."

I rubbed my forehead. The reality was that my dream of zipping back to America in the blink of an eye was flawed. I had to listen to Mom, whether or not she meant her words.

When the line clicked, I broke down. I was helpless, half a world away from Mom. I could not make her better here, or there. But each moment I spent on this trip meant one less moment with her.

A few hours later, in a local market in Pushkar, I was trailing at the end of our tour group as we wandered through the packed, one-lane street lined with tents and tables that displayed finely woven rugs, knitted socks, little Hindu statues, and boxes of multi-colored beads. I stared absently at the merchants pushing and pressing against each other, shouting as they fought to sell their goods. The smoke and steam from the stewing curry and the barbecuing vegetables, mixed with the lingering stench of hashish following the throng of moving bodies—all of it engulfed my face, suffocating me.

In the midst of the crowd, I was drawn to an elderly woman carrying a basket of straw. Nothing in particular about her appearance struck me—she stood less than five feet tall, with weathered skin and long gray hair flowing down her back. But her aura radiated peace. I felt compelled to go over to her. As I did, two boys ran between us and knocked her over, sending her and her basket to the ground.

The boys kept running, laughing about what they had done. My hand and heart raced as I rushed to help the woman up. Her eyes darted from my hands to my face—shock at my blonde hair and fair skin. But then she squeezed my hand and smiled, nodding continuously as I lifted her to her feet. I bent down, collected the fallen straw into her basket, and placed it back into her arms.

We stared at each other, unable to speak a word of the other's language. But her eyes engulfed me in warmth, expressing her thanks. She was someone's mother or grand-mother—I just knew.

As the woman walked away, I remembered Mom's travel crystal tucked away in my purse. I pulled the crystal out of the silk pouch and held it up. I looked deeply into the prisms of dancing light, then around at the market place. The colors seemed more alive—more vibrant—than I knew colors could be. Was it possible that, amid the angst of all this helplessness, a piece of me was waking up?

Chapter 5: Accept Authenticity

November

I steered the golden turkey—perfectly cooked—from the oven to its serving platter. I smiled proudly at Mom, who shuffled around behind me, checking each side dish. She would find nothing lacking in her traditional Thanksgiving feast.

"How's the gravy coming, Dad?" I called. And with Mom right across from me, I performed my usual ritual, plucking a piece of steaming, crispy skin from the side of the turkey and popping it into my mouth.

"Mmm," I hummed, but Mom continued to check the side dishes.

No scolding? I thought.

The act of snitching skin off the turkey was an annual game. How much skin could we eat before Mom told us to stop?

Dad skirted around me into the kitchen.

"Here, Dad, have some," I said louder than usual, pinching off another piece of crispy skin. I watched Mom as he took it. Not even a glance.

An uncharacteristic pressure began building in the air as we put the finishing touches on our Thanksgiving meal. Everything was as it should be—the large turkey, stuffing, mashed potatoes and gravy, bright red cranberry relish, refrigerator rolls, and pumpkin pie spread across the expansive dining room table. Yet, all was not as it should be—the oxygen tank nestled beside Mom's chair, the minuscule amount of food on her plate, and, in the lulls of conversation, her soft, labored breathing.

The comforting clinking of silverware on plates eased us into the meal. "Mom, this is so delicious," my sister said of the homemade food. All the dishes were Mom's recipes. However, this year, Mom hadn't made any of it. We hid the truth with nods and smiles.

"Why don't we say what we're thankful for?" my sister added.

Dad started. He was grateful for our family, for the food, and our blessed lives. My younger daughter echoed his sentiment, and then my brother-in-law cracked his token inappropriate joke before agreeing.

Mom sat at one head of the table, across from Dad. It was her turn next. My daughters and nephews asked, "What are you grateful for, Nana?"

She stared down her plate, the muscles in her cheeks twitching, as if some part of her wanted to hold back the answer. My teeth clamped as the word came out of her mouth. "Nothing," she said. And then she started to cry.

The pressure in the room expanded like a too-full balloon. I could count on the fingers of one hand how many times I had seen Mom cry in my entire life. Every face around the table drained of color, eyes wide with shock. I sat dumbfounded for a long moment, until Dad jumped up and rushed to Mom's side. I followed as my sister reached over and took Mom's hand, her lips trembling.

Mom kept her head tilted down, tears dripping from the edge of her cheeks. I placed my hand on her back, gripping slightly as if I could pull her up from this dark place.

I had tried so hard to make this meal the way our family had done it for years—the way Mom had done it. But today Mom did not want to hide behind the perfect meal.

Her tears revealed that everything was changing, and there was nothing any of us could do about it.

"I'm so sorry, Mom," I said.

Dad caught my eye with a sharp look.

I pressed my lips together, not daring to say anything else.

After a few minutes, Mom's tears subsided. We all resumed our seats. The children averted their gazes to their plates, still full of food. We picked and prodded at that perfect meal for a while longer, none of us talking, all of us absorbing the awful truth.

As dinner ended, everyone migrated to the family room and hid behind watching a movie. My sister and I, for the first time, took refuge in doing all the dishes.

I dropped the leftover turkey into plastic bags and then addressed the residue-laden platter. We had lovingly used this platter for every holiday and special occasion. Cleaned it time and time again, put it away dutifully, fully knowing it would serve us another day.

This platter, this place, was supposed to be home. And yet I felt a dull ache in my heart—homesick for what was slipping away. Our family was changing. And there was nothing I could do to stop it. The rules weren't working anymore, not for Mom, not for any of us.

My sister's hand took the other end of the platter. "I'll dry it."

I relinquished it to her and whispered, "I hope Mom gets to use it again."

Her hand moved in careful circles across the illustrated horse-drawn sleigh and snow-covered cabins. "Me too," she said.

Together we slid the platter back into the cabinet and shut the door, enclosing it once again in darkness.

Chapter 6: Let Them Lead

December

" *J* feel like, well, like I'm burning," Mom said. Sweat dripped down her cherry-red face. The makeup she had applied early that morning now seeped into her pillowcase. She kicked the blanket off her legs for the umpteenth time, struggling to sit up. I put a throw pillow behind her back for support, then reached for the half-eaten cracker on the table and held it out to her. She cringed and exhaled a quivering breath through her pursed lips.

I had never seen Mom like this, so vulnerable, undone.

"Still nauseous?" I asked.

She nodded and slumped to lie back down.

Five years into Mom's disease, the doctor had suggested a regimen of chemotherapy, despite her not having cancer, in hopes that it would slow the scarring of her lung tissue. According to the doctor, this was the only viable treatment for Mom. Unfortunately, the side effects of the drug were taking a toll. Now the pain she felt was nearly unbearable. And her misery was my misery. I did not want her on the medicine anymore, but I could not make the decision for her.

I had set up my parents' matching wicker loveseats in the den with pillows and blankets, creating bed-like comfort. I sat in a little chair firmly beside Mom with a washcloth in hand. I dipped it into a bowl of ice water, wrung it out, and gently patted her burning cheeks.

She looked at me like an abused dog in a kennel. "I don't know if I can do this anymore. If this is what my life will be like . . ."

Her words struck me like a surreal déjà vu; almost twenty years ago I had felt the same uncertainty for a very different reason.

I had just graduated from college and begun studying for the daunting nursing board exam, the last obstacle standing between me and a nursing career.

I had heard the horror stories. Hours in a hot, crowded auditorium surrounded by hundreds of other nervous test takers. Tricky multiple-choice questions scrambled to quiz you on the kidneys, then the cardiovascular system, and then infections. No rhyme or reason.

I was already working long hours at the local hospital as a medical assistant and was a newlywed—so I was sneaking in my studying any chance I could get.

The day before exam day I made the tiring, two-hour trek to Los Angeles. My friends were piled in the back of my car, relaxing while I drove, alert and anxious. After eight grueling hours in the exam auditorium, we had walked zombie-like out into the starry evening and crammed back into my car. Driving home I was exhausted, but so relieved it was over.

All there was to do now was wait.

A few weeks later, that envelope from the Board of Registered Nurses showed up. I stood on the curb and tore it open with shaking hands, my heart fluttering. And there it stated:

Failed.

Five measly points stood between me and my nursing career. Devastation weighed me down as I sank onto the curb and cried. All my friends were waiting to hear that I had received the same good news they had. They were ready to celebrate their budding careers. And there I was—left behind. Knowing that all I had to look forward to was another six months of studying and that harrowing exam—again.

"I don't know if I can do it, Mom," I confessed later that day on the phone.

"Lannette, tomorrow you get the paperwork in order. You sign up for that test the very next time they offer it."

"But what if I do all that studying again and don't pass?"

"In the long run, no one will know or remember when you passed your exam. It'll all just be a distant memory."

Her words fueled my motivation for the next six months. I got a whole new set of study guides, made new flash cards, and created sayings and analogies to help me remember the concepts. (What are the five stages of grief? DABDA: Denial, Anger, Bargaining, Depression, Acceptance.)

This time, no friends were relaxing in the back of my car. This time, I was in the passenger seat, with Mom at the wheel. This time, we stayed in a nice hotel a couple blocks away. The next morning, Mom planted herself outside the large auditorium and read a book all day, as if there were no other place in the world she would rather be. After the grueling day, I walked out of the auditorium and fell into Mom's smiling embrace.

This time, I had the exam results sent to Mom's house. And two weeks later, she was at my door with an envelope in her hand from the Board of Registered Nurses. Anxiety tightened my chest. What if I didn't pass—again?

She confidently handed me the envelope and I held my breath as I opened it. And there it stated:

Congratulations.

Mom smiled over at me. "Well, it looks like you're officially a registered nurse."

Mom panted through a grimace as I re-dipped the washcloth. Whether or not I could decide for her, I had to know what she wanted. I dropped the washcloth and held her hand. "Whatever you want to do, I'm here." I bit my lip, and then pushed the words out clearly. "Do you want off the medicine?"

"Yes," she whispered.

"Okay then, we can get you off of it."

She looked up at me with glassy eyes. "And you'll still be here?"

"Mom, I'm not going anywhere."

The worry wrinkle between her brows relaxed, and she melted back onto the couch. She kept hold of my hand and I kept hold of hers. But my heart ached in her relief. Though neither of us would say it, we both knew going off the drug meant less time. Mom was choosing to surrender, to enjoy the days she had left instead of fighting for more. And I wondered what that meant for our remaining time together—what life would look like without the fight.

Chapter 7: Be a Sanctuary

Early January

Most days, no wind blew through the hills behind my parents' house. I hadn't noticed this stillness before; the overwhelming bustle of movement had distracted from the serenity. Now there was much less movement with just Mom and me, and her energy level was sharply declining.

Some part of my brain was still focused on my to-do list, yet, as the days went by, I found myself gravitating toward the den, toward Mom. We would sit there facing one another, the yard just within sight.

Mom and I had never done this together, just sitting quietly. No end goal of making a meal or sending thank you cards or planning a birthday party. And one day, Mom began to fill the silence.

She had never been the type to chatter on about her life. She kept her thoughts and emotions in check. But the more attentive I became, the more her words flowed. Her expression told me she was appreciative I was there, willing to listen. As her words tumbled out, a different side of her blossomed before my eyes. I began to feel less like a daughter and more like a friend. A sense of magic rolled into the space as Mom shared stories I'd never heard before.

She painted a picture of her home life as a young girl on the west side of Albuquerque, New Mexico. It was a small, dusty place with a failing post-depression economy. Her father was a grocery store owner, but after giving food on credit to so many people—who never had the money to pay him back—the store went out of business, and he became a construction worker. He held odd jobs, but her mother was the main breadwinner with a steady job in a restaurant bar. Consequently, she was gone most afternoons and often deep into the night.

Though the second oldest of five siblings, Mom was the one taking care of things. She explained that their home had two bedrooms and one bathroom. She and her three sisters shared one bedroom. Her little brother slept in the adjoining room with her parents. The rooms were sparsely furnished with mattresses on the floor. Each of her siblings had a shoebox that contained all of their personal items.

"I cherished that box," she said, "and would keep it neatly tucked away."

It was a small home, crowded with necessity and survival—with only enough room for the important questions. Would there be food on the table tomorrow? How would they get new shoes after they grew out of the old ones? Who would stay home from school to watch the little ones that day?

I imagined that life in that house was slow or boring, but Mom shared that it was often very busy, with people coming and going, mainly men passing through town who needed a place to stay.

Mom paused and lowered her eyes to her hands, which were moving back and forth along the edge of the blanket that covered her. I could tell she was about to say something important.

"One time something happened," she said, "and I hid in the bedroom closet."

She cleared her throat and looked at me with steely eyes. My mind began to fill in the blanks of exactly what could have led her to that closet, but there was something in her expression that subdued my curiosity. In that instant I knew that as a very little girl, Mom had been hurt.

She explained how she decided to retreat into the closet and not come out until someone came to get her.

Hours passed. Nothing.

Day turned to night. Nothing.

And then it became clear. No one was looking for her. No one was coming to get her.

Late that night, she opened the door and a feeling washed over her that she would never shake. It was the realization that she was truly on her own in the world. That it would be foolish to depend on anyone else, and that the only one who would take care of her was she herself.

The next day a plan was born within her—she devised the book of rules that would get her out of that life of poverty.

As I listened to her story, I had a feeling this was one of the only times she had talked about the closet incident. The secret she divulged was not the terrible event that led her to the closet, but that she had sat there waiting for help that never came. It was a secret that explained so much—why she was not particularly outwardly affectionate or emotionally available. She was not one to shower you with hugs and kisses. Hers was a quiet, yet solid kind of love. True and real, protective and steadfast.

Mom had so passionately loved and protected us, even though—or maybe because—no one had protected her.

Chapter 8: Remember to Look Up

Mid-January

*T*he leaves blew in small funnels in the street, the afternoon breeze whistling a happy tune over our car as Mom and I headed home from the doctor. Inside the car the air was stale, magnified by the beating sun on the dashboard, but the air conditioning or a rolled-down window would irritate Mom's cough. So we processed the doctor's news in stuffy silence. Mom's walking days were coming to an end. And she knew it.

Mom looked over at me for the first time since leaving the doctor's office. "Can we stop by the card shop?"

I didn't ask why, I just nodded and turned the car around. I knew the place well. It was a colorful shop in a tiny strip mall. Nothing fancy, but it was hers.

Craving normalcy, we chatted like it was any other day—about dinner, the weather, hairstyles. When we arrived, the parking lot was nearly full. I looked around, growing concerned. Not a handicap spot in sight. Mom was too weak to walk very far, so I circled around again. And then in her most nonchalant voice she said, "Just pull up to the curb." She pointed to the brightly painted, *very red* curb at the front of the store. "I'll just run in and you can wait in the car."

I hesitated. Mom wasn't running anywhere, and I wanted to walk with her, but what could I do? I nodded and pulled up to the curb. She unbuckled her seat belt with fumbling hands. Her breathing labored, she struggled to open the car door. I jumped out and ran around. Gingerly, together, we maneuvered so that each of her feet was firmly planted on the sidewalk. I grabbed her oxygen bag. She stood up a little straighter and caught her breath. I held her arm and began to walk in with her.

"No," she said. "I." Breath. "Will." Breath. "Go." Breath. "In." Breath. "Myself."

Like a young mom watching her kindergartener trundle off to school, I watched Mom make her way into the store. *I want just a bit of my independence*, I could hear her soul saying to me.

I gritted my teeth against the worries in my mind— my car parked illegally, the possibility of Mom falling or hyperventilating, the other chores I had left undone.

I held myself back as she shuffled her feet until she was able to pull the door open.

The store's windows were large and uncovered, so I could see inside from my sidewalk perch. The shop seemed to be free of other people, except for the clueless female employee at the register.

The girl did not acknowledge Mom as she slowly walked around with a smile on her face. The girl, like so many of us, was caught up in her own world. She had no idea that this could be the last time Mom visited this store, or any other.

I peered a little closer as Mom picked up a card that flashed silver, and a memory flooded over me.

It was a warm Southern California night, and Mom was leading us onto the darkened beach. I was ten and my sister was six. We were tightly bundled in layers of shirts and jackets. The stars sparkled above us. Mom carried a big basket filled with a thermos of hot chocolate, mugs, and a blanket. Softly, as we walked, she explained, "Only a few months out of the year, these silver, slender fish make their way onto the sandy beaches to lay their eggs. It's called a grunion run!"

We looked out onto the empty sand, a blank canvas.

"But I don't see anything; when will they come?" I asked.

"Soon," Mom said. "Let's just enjoy our hot chocolate for now."

My sister and I knew this was a special night. Not only did we get to miss school the next morning (because, yes, this was an educational experience in and of itself), but she was teaching us how to pause.

Life had become hectic in our little house: school, homework, chores, work, meals, more chores. We lived by the clock. But tonight we were living by nature's timing. We carefully set up our blankets on the upper part of the beach, just out of range of the wet sand.

With no manmade lights to be seen, the moonlight illuminated each wave that rolled in. As they crashed, Mom opened the thermos full of hot chocolate, and steam danced out into the cold air. She poured us each a full mug, and within a few minutes the beach began to glow. Sprinkles of silver glistened in the waves.

"Mom, I see something!"

"Look over there!" we shouted, as these delicate, shiny creatures surfed in with each wave, splashing in the hundreds onto the sand in front of us. We giggled with delight, not believing our eyes.

Soon the entire beach was shimmering with silver movement. We looked up and noticed that a small crowd had gathered above us to take in the magical sight. In awe we observed as the grunion flipped and burrowed into the sand to lay their eggs. I turned to look up at Mom, her eyes twinkling. I was so proud that she was my mom—that while all the other parents were tucking their children into bed, she had brought us to the beach to experience the invisible beauty in the world.

A car whooshed by, sending a wave of warm air over me. I opened my eyes to find my car was still in the red hazard zone, Mom still meandering inside the shop.

And I realized that she had done this my whole life—tried to teach me to pause.

In a way, my mom's illness had placed my whole life on pause, and I found that as my movements slowed down, these precious, singular memories long suppressed were now emerging.

I raised my face to the cloudless blue sky and breathed in the light breeze. I no longer cared if I got a ticket. This moment was just as it should be.

I heard Mom shuffling and met her gaze as she neared. She reached for my hand and I noticed she held no bag—she hadn't purchased a thing.

Chapter 9: Find Your Ritual

Late January

*I*n the hallway past my parents' kitchen, tucked away on a wall barely wide enough to accommodate it, was a wood and glass antique armoire that housed Mom's most prized possessions—her teacups. Collected one by one, year by year, on trips around the world and as gifts from loved ones, each displayed a unique flower design and nestled atop a matching saucer. Sprinkled throughout the cups were miniature cream pitchers and delicate sugar bowls. All of them locked away until Mom approved their use.

In the pantry across from the armoire sat a wooden box adorned with colorful painted fruits. It was always left open, inviting passersby to pluck a bag of chamomile or Earl Grey tea from its midst. And when they did, Mom would take out her teacups. When formal entertaining ceased, when there were no more outings, when walking became difficult and breathing was labor, teatime became a way for Mom to socialize.

Before Mom's diagnosis, I had always rushed to slop coffee or tea in a mug and scramble off to work. I couldn't remember one time I had savored the experience as Mom had. Yet now, on any given day, Mom's sister or a good friend brought their uplifting smiles and warming spirits into the den for teatime, and the ritual unfolded:

1. Take out the serving tray.
2. Place Mom's tea box on the tray.
3. Heat the water in the kettle.
4. Select the cups.
5. Pour the water into the teacups.
6. Ever so carefully, carry the portable tea station into the den and place it on the coffee table.
7. Meet Mom's eyes as she smiled, knowing the next few minutes would be savored.

Mom had never been a conversationalist. Yet as she sipped, a small window into her world opened.

Looking at a teacup, she would recount how, when, and where that particular cup had been purchased. Once I heard her rhapsodize about a cup that she'd brought home from Iceland. It was white with pastel paint strokes flowing from base to tip. She loved it because the colors reminded her of the beautiful reflection of the sun off the clouds and the ocean's surface; a sideways rainbow, she called it.

As Mom and her company enjoyed their tea, I often stepped into the kitchen to prepare dinner. I wanted teatime to be their private time, just as it had been before this detour. While I chopped and cooked, I bathed in the sound of their laughter. For just a moment, I could breathe deeply, my chest and shoulders relaxed, taking in the positive energy that would keep me moving forward.

As a nurse, I had seen it go so differently. I knew all too well that end-of-life care could turn into a dark place, where people enter to cry, complain, pity the suffering, mourn the slipping away . . . Yet, here was Mom, even in the toughest moments, sitting upright, sipping her tea, cracking up her best friend.

Chapter 10: Maybe You Can't Walk but You Can Roll

February

The patter of February rain taunted us as Mom struggled to put one foot in front of the other. Her shortened breaths rivaled the speed of the falling water drops outside, until it was too much. Mom pursed her lips, rattled breath volleying in and out, and gripped the back of a dining room chair. I hurriedly helped her into it.

She shook her head. "It's too far."

I gritted my teeth, fighting the pressure in my chest. The laughter from *The Ellen Show* broadcasting in the other room magnified the undeniable truth: it was time for a wheelchair.

Mom's eyes were full of dread. To accept this fact meant to accept that she was getting worse, that she would now have to rely on it—and others—to get around.

For a week, Mom had been talking about visiting her boat. About a year earlier, Mom had encouraged Dad to upgrade to a forty-eight-foot yacht. Though both of them knew where she was in her diagnosis, and Mom did not particularly like boating, Dad had complied. It gave Mom peace to know he had a fun hobby to look forward to. And now visiting the boat was a means of breaking our solitary routine.

I was determined to find a way to make it happen.

On a day Dad stayed home, I snuck out of their house to complete the first step: acquiring transport. In the back right corner of our local pharmacy, beside the canes and walkers, was a row of wheelchairs. As I walked down the aisle, each one seemed more depressing than the last, until I caught sight of the one at the end. It was bright cherry red. I shrugged. If she was going to have a wheelchair, it might as well be fancy. I rolled it out happily, knowing it would become Mom's chariot.

When we arrived at their yacht club, the first thing I noticed was the warming sun shining down on the water. The second thing I noticed was the large ramp that we would need to descend to get from the club grounds to the boat docks. The docks were built to sit just above the water line and rise and fall with the tide, and the time of day we happened to choose for our visit was at low tide, so that the ramp was almost upright. It might as well have been a slide—not like a child's slide at the park, more like the giant ones they have at the fair. I quickly scanned the docks. There had to be someone walking by who could help us. Nope. Not a soul. Mom had, of course, consciously chosen a slow time so she could slip in and out unnoticed.

So, there we were: Mom, me, the ridiculously steep ramp, and the bright red wheelchair.

As I rolled Mom carefully onto the ramp's edge, we both looked straight down. There were only a few feet between safety and a whole lot of water.

"Here we go," I said cheerfully, yet all I could think

was, *Oh no—what if I lose my grasp, what if the chair flies free and Mom careens right into the water?*

My nerves shot up, my heart raced, and Mom clutched the wheelchair armrests.

I can do this. I can do this for Mom, I chanted internally.

We began at a slow glide down the steep incline. With every bump that the wheels hit, a jolt shot through us. About halfway down I realized that my momentum was almost too fast to stop. In an attempt to control my nerves, I blurted, "We're doing great."

To which she replied, "Yep, yep."

As we neared the end of the ramp, I leaned as far back as I could without losing my grip on the chair. We both heaved a sigh of relief as it came to a stop just shy of the water.

I'd done it. I'd brought Mom to the boat.

"I'd like to go on it," she said.

I swallowed hard, wondering how in the world I would make that happen. Suddenly getting down the ramp seemed like the easy part.

But if she was determined, then so was I. I rolled Mom over to the boat and pulled it as close to the edge of the dock as possible. Then we made slow, deliberate micro-movements and shimmied her tiny frame onto the boat.

As soon as she was safely on, we exhaled. Mom's face lit up like a child at sea for the first time. The wind was soft, and the water gently lapped around us. I realized in that moment how much life she still had in her.

We huddled together for a snack of cheese and crackers. In some ways it felt like any other afternoon with Mom. And yet, I could hear her struggling to breathe.

The salty breeze hid the tears trying to spill over my cheeks. We had moved farther down the bridge, but this time we had rolled.

Chapter 11: Accept the Torch

March

As my sister and nephews shopped, Mom sat in her bright red wheelchair in the middle of the boys' clothing section of our local department store. Their blonde hair bobbed up and down between the racks as they searched for the perfect outfits. Mom looked on with quiet joy. Their happiness was her happiness.

Mom had created this tradition years earlier when my two girls were little. My younger daughter had dubbed it a shopping outing at "the escalator store." Mom wanted to make sure her grandchildren had what they needed as the seasons changed, and the department store had everything, so four times a year, Mom scheduled an outing there.

My preadolescent nephews, who were just starting to understand brand names, ran up to show Mom their prizes. They babbled on, justifying the importance of their selections, clearly seeing past the wheelchair. All that mattered was that Nana was there.

Mom handed me the credit card, and I took the boys to the counter to pay. Out of the corner of my eye, I noticed tears winding a path down her cheeks. She wiped them off swiftly with the back of her hand, not wanting anyone to see.

"Why don't you guys ride down the escalator, and we'll meet you at the door!" I said to my nephews, with as much enthusiasm as I could muster. I threw my sister an earnest look as the boys shouted "Yeah!" She nodded in understanding.

My knees wobbled as I wheeled Mom toward the elevator. I caught our reflection in one of the mirror columns. My shoulders were hunched. Her slight frame slumped against the seat back. This was so different from the mom I knew growing up.

When I was in the ninth grade, my family moved, and I had to transfer schools three weeks into the semester. I left all my friends behind, and it was too late to join a sports team or a club. I was in the awkward teenage years where nothing fit right, and I did not really know who I was. I felt like I didn't belong anywhere.

At my new school, half the student body was in a gang, and the other half just did not seem to care. My geography teacher could barely control the unruly crowd. He was Santa Claus in plain clothing, as wide as he was tall, with pasty skin so light that it almost glowed. But there was nothing jolly about him or his class. Kids talked over him. Spit wads flew across the room. All the while, I sat there, locked in silent confusion.

I had caught up on my schoolwork, but it seemed I couldn't do anything right. If a spit wad came near my desk, the teacher pinned it on me. If there was any whispering or talking, he yelled at me to behave. Though I diligently did all of my homework and studied hard for his tests, I could garner nothing higher than a C or D. For some reason, this man was bent on failing me.

Mom listened and watched silently as I struggled to meet the teacher's standards. Mid-semester, when I brought home my progress report, she said only one thing: "What time does geography class start and in what room?"

The next day when I walked down the hallway, Mom was standing outside the classroom.

"Mom, what are you doing here?" I asked.

She placed her hand on my shoulder and said, "Let's go in."

She sat down at the desk beside me, without another word. The teacher entered the room and when he registered Mom's presence, shock turned his pasty skin even whiter. His thoughts were palpable: *What is this mother doing here, in his class?*

Mom did not get up to say hello, did not move to shake his hand or explain herself. Without fully acknowledging the teacher, she kept her eyes on him as he stumbled through his lesson with shaky hands and voice. And when the bell rang, Mom got up and walked out beside me.

From that day on, the teacher never accused me of whispering secrets behind his back or shooting spitballs. He barely even called on me. My grades went up to A's and B's, finally reflecting my hard work.

Apparently, no words had been needed. While another mother might have held a parent–teacher conference or given the teacher a piece of her mind and forced him into submission, my mom had moved mountains without ever making a sound.

Now Mom's silence was very different. As we waited beside the baby-filled strollers and young moms for the elevator doors to open, there was no strength in her posture. Her frail shoulders sank forward, her hands rested heavily in her lap, her legs relaxed to one side.

When those grey doors finally opened, the young moms pushed their way in first. I maneuvered Mom beside their strollers. The laughter and movement from the babies magnified Mom's inactivity. The beginning and end of the life cycle surrounded me.

Mom strained to look up at me. "I know you will continue to do this with the boys," she said.

My throat cinched, and a sense of responsibility settled over me in that tiny, claustrophobic space. This was not just about taking my nephews shopping. Mom was anticipating the holes she would leave in her wake—the holes that our family would need filled. She was asking me to fill them, to become the strong presence that, day-by-day, was diminishing in her. It was an understated passing of the torch—our eyes never even met. But she had extended it, and I found myself standing up a little straighter.

As the doors opened, so did something deep within me; a newfound strength filled my heart. "Of course I will, Mom."

Chapter 12: Slow Down with Fast Food

April

As we drove around looking for a place to eat, all I could think of was wrestling with the cherry red wheelchair, Mom's short breaths, the strain on her face— all for a sandwich or something I could make her at home. Nevertheless, ladies' lunch was what we did, and this would not be the day we could no longer do it.

I pointed out a few options along the dull, concrete street, and Mom mumbled with distracted indifference.

Then her finger shot out, pointing past the gas station ahead. Her voice rang with excitement as she said, "Let's eat there!"

It was a Burger King.

Really?

Mom was not a fast food lady. She made all meals from scratch, used all natural ingredients, and frowned upon anyone else eating in what she deemed as an unhealthy manner. But today fast food was a heaven-sent option.

We pulled up to the drive-through menu. Mom read carefully, cheerfully, before making her selection—a Whopper Junior. Of course Mom ordered the smallest hamburger on the menu, even now still watching her calorie intake.

We drove through, picked up our lunch, and pulled out into the parking lot. There was only one space available, butted up against the sidewalk—the border between us and the rest of the world. Just outside the window, life was everywhere. A couple on bright blue bicycles coasted across the street, a young mom pushing a heavy stroller with one hand pulled her feisty toddler along with the other, an old man followed his dog around a thick palm tree.

Everyone was walking—everyone but us.

Pressure built behind my eyes. I swallowed and looked down, unwrapping Mom's hamburger.

How did we get here?

I glanced over to Mom's reflection in the window, and memories flooded in.

Hot August afternoons after horseback riding, my sister and I plopping into the back seat of the beige, paneled Country Squire station wagon. Pulling into the drive-through to get the biggest, fattest, juiciest hot dog on the menu—the Polish Dog—washed down with icy sodas. Nothing tasted so good. Chattering away about the horses, the bumpy trails, the jokes we shared in the barn. Mom handing us our food, her smile reflecting the joy she felt watching and listening, never eating anything herself.

And now, forty years later, she had an entirely different grin on her face. Looking out the window, watching the yapping dog run by, the trees bowing to the heat of the desert sun, and eating a hamburger. Simply enjoying a hamburger.

And I was beside her. Awake to every sound and scent. Taking another step across the bridge. In a Burger King parking lot.

Chapter 13: Let Your Heart
Speak to Other Hearts

May

Spring was right outside the window. The sky was blue and cloudless. The hills were covered in lush greenery from all the recent rain. Roses blossomed in the garden, their sweet smell filling the air. Mom and I admired it all from the family room, through the screen door.

"I have an idea," Mom said, peering with half-lidded eyes out the window. "Let's take a drive out to the coast."

I quickly agreed. Any time I could see that spark of life in her eyes, I wanted to fan the flames, to help her feel part of the flow of daily life. What I did not realize was that Mom had another reason—or maybe a purpose—for wanting to make this trip.

As I prepared the wheelchair and oxygen line, she casually asked about my mother-in-law. "Why don't you call and see if she's around for a visit?"

I tried to hide my shock. My mother-in-law and Mom were not exactly good friends. In fact, I could not remember the two of them ever having a real conversation. My husband, our girls, and I spent most holidays either with my side of the family or with his, but very rarely both together. In addition, I wondered how this visit could work, since Mom would probably be unable to enter the split-level house with its medley of stairs. I did not understand, yet I knew if Mom had asked, it was important to her. So without questioning, I made the phone call, and then we headed for the coast.

About an hour later, I pulled the car into my mother-in-law's driveway. The front door was already cracked open—she was waiting to meet us, perhaps knowing that it would be difficult for Mom to get out of the car.

The next few moments played out for me as if in slow motion. My mother-in-law, a designer sweat suit adorning her tall, thin frame, slipped through the open door and approached us. Her jet-black hair, the same length as Mom's, was perfectly flipped under to hit just above her chin.

Mom rolled down her window. My mother-in-law reached an olive-skinned hand through and Mom took it. The two women—years of history and grandchildren between them—smiled.

"Oh, it's so good to see you," my mother-in-law said softly, her brown eyes widening in genuine greeting.

Mom's blue eyes lit up in response. "It's wonderful to be here."

They made small talk, chatting about the latest event my mother-in-law had attended, how fast their granddaughters (my two girls) were maturing, what my husband was up to. I could see how hard they were trying to keep the conversation light and upbeat, to keep it flowing without pause.

I remained silent; this conversation was just for the two of them. Within the small talk, an invisible gap was mending. Two people who had existed for so long on the periphery of each other's lives were now face to face, connecting, knowing each other, maybe for the first time.

After about twenty minutes, I could sense Mom growing tired. My mother-in-law seemed to notice too, and said, "Next time I'll make a bite to eat, and we can visit over a snack."

"Well, you know I always love your tuna salad," Mom said.

"Then tuna it will be."

They shared a smile. Mom's breath became shorter. I wondered if my mother-in-law knew there would be no next visit, no tuna salad.

"You ready to get going, Mom?" I asked.

Her breathing still labored, Mom turned and looked directly into my mother-in-law's eyes. And in that moment, these two graceful, strong-willed matriarchs broke the barrier of distant connection they'd held onto for years. "Please love and be there for my granddaughters."

My breath hitched in my throat, my lips parting in shock. I looked to my mother-in-law, who agreed to this promise with a solemn nod.

As the shock subsided on our drive home, I gave in to the sadness and joy swirling in my heart. That Mom loved me and my girls so much that she'd made the hour-long drive just for that one request. And that Mom needed and wanted to make the request herself—that she was so worried my mother-in-law would not be there for us and wanted to be certain. It left me speechless. I didn't know it at the time, but her words would echo in my heart for years to come.

Chapter 14: Handle the Things You Can

Early June

"*I* feel nauseous," Mom sputtered.

Hair done, makeup applied, sweat suit perfectly pressed, she sat in the car's passenger seat with her hands folded in her lap. Mom's sisters were in town from New Mexico—a special trip they had planned with the intention of visiting her as much as possible. But after a draining family reunion the day before, I knew lunch at my cousin's house was going to be too much.

We were driving to the fork in the road that joined the path from Mom's house to my aunt's house, and Mom's face was getting paler and paler, her breath shorter and shorter. Soon she was hyperventilating.

My heart quickened. This was exactly what I had been afraid of.

My aunt's car was still making its way up the adjacent road, but there was no time to wait. I U-turned and floored it back to my parents' driveway two hundred feet away.

I had barely put the car in park and cut the engine when Mom pushed her door open with a wheeze, hands and legs trembling below her body weight.

I opened my door and ran around the back to reach her. "Hold on, Mom, let me help you."

My hands met with her shaking body as I pulled her to her feet. We tried to make it to the house, but the thirty-foot stretch between the car and the walkway seemed to expand before us, the front door just outside our grasp.

Unable to walk any further, Mom collapsed and vomited. I knelt down with her, trying to support her so she was not lying on the lawn. As she wretched and heaved, gasping for air, my own stomach churned. This was my *mom*. The person who had held me in her arms and picked me up each time I fell. Now she couldn't even stand.

I looked behind me, to my aunts in their car, which sat at the end of the driveway. I knew Mom would not want them to see her like this, so I waved for them to leave.

I gathered up Mom, and we walked the final few feet toward her home. Mom's housekeeper ran out and helped me walk her in. We got her settled onto the bed. I cleaned her up, wiped her brow, and offered her water.

"I don't know why this happened," she said, "I just don't know why."

Then she drifted off to sleep.

I did know why. My heart hung heavy in my chest as I crept from the room.

My voice quivered on the phone with Mom's personal doctor. I filled him in on the symptoms and on how Mom was coping. The empathy in his voice nearly snapped the thin threads holding me together.

"I think we're at the end," he said. "I'll refer you to hospice. It's time to call them."

I placed the phone back on the wall, and then sank into one of the dining room chairs, finally allowing the tears to come. My breath hiccupped out of me as I stared at the ticking grandfather clock while I waited for Dad. An overwhelming feeling of homesickness engulfed my body.

I wanted to hold on, to cling to my mother's hands, to stop time. I knew that calling in hospice meant that there would be no more efforts toward keeping Mom alive, only care to offer her comfort, to help her die with the least pain possible.

I did not bother to hide my tears when Dad got home. He faltered at the front door, his face growing pale as he took in my appearance. Together we made the call neither of us ever wanted to make. Defeat thickened the air. We listened with shortened breaths to the subdued, calming female voice on the other end as she walked us through the steps of making an assessment appointment.

After the call was completed, we went and sat next to Mom. Her eyes were shut, her face relaxed, at peace. There were no wrinkles indicating she was trying to keep her eyes open. It was the first time she had given into her exhaustion, and I was struck by how this made her appear less in her body than before, as if a piece of her were hovering somewhere just out of reach.

Chapter 15: Know Your Limits

Mid-June

The doorbell rang, slicing through the tension in the air. Dad's eyes met mine before he moved toward the door, where four strangers stood silhouetted in the stained glass. Opening that door meant relinquishing the privacy and self-reliance our family had maintained our whole lives. But it also meant getting the help we needed.

I stood beside Mom, who sat on the couch with her hands in her lap, wearing a mask of calm and ease. Her complexion as glowing as ever, she was the picture of health and grace. Inside I was shaking, because though she did not look sick, she *was* sick. Her heart rate was as fast as a hummingbird's wings, her blood pressure almost double what it should be, and her breathing so rapid she could have rivaled the fastest marathon runner. The medication she would need daily to manage her anxiety and pain was now beyond what we could provide.

As Dad led the hospice team inside, Mom greeted them with her beautiful smile. The doctor and nurses made their way to the armchairs circling the coffee table.

We gathered around them and our introduction to hospice began. The doctor explained that hospice was a shift in care, one that was geared toward the dying process. So focused was I on Mom, I did not hear exactly what he said next, but her face brightened and she asked, "So I can graduate from hospice?" The hope in her eyes made my heart clench.

The doctor nodded. I knew doctors, and I knew this one did not think that Mom was as ill as we had expressed. I could almost hear his thoughts: *How could that healthy-looking woman be so close to death?*

As the doctor examined her, Mom did her best to look and sound physically well. He listened to her heart and lungs and watched her breathing. She knew how to keep her respirations and heart rate down for a short time. The doctor nodded, as if to say, *not too bad.*

My stomach turned upside down. I wanted to scream. *Please do not leave us!*

Just an hour before, I had listened helplessly to Mom nearly hyperventilating after taking just a few steps to reach a chair. A scene of Mom being rolled onto an ambulance from a heart attack—or worse—played over and over in my head.

We had done everything in our power to keep her home, in comfort, and we were not going to give up now. But here she was, putting on a show for this doctor. What was it going to take for her to realize that she needed their help?

As a little girl, I frequented a wonderful riding stable down the hill from my house called the Red Barn. It looked like it came out of a storybook, with the bright red barn, outdoor horse stalls, and riding rings. The ground was all dirt, and I loved everything about it. Behind the barn were large Eucalyptus trees lining whimsical trails. I was free to ride them alone to my heart's content.

I had a pony horse named King Louie. Just as it sounds, he was not big enough to be considered a horse and not small enough to be a pony, but he was perfect for me. He was silky black from head to hoof, and his long tail and mane waved as we moved, no matter how strong the wind. His forelock, the hair that hung between his eyes, almost reached the opening of his nares.

One afternoon when I was riding King Louie, a noise spooked him, and he sent me flying onto the dusty trail. I hit the ground—hard—and King Louie ran past my friends who were ahead of me. As the air sputtered back into my lungs, panic rose within me. I was too winded to chase after him. Every second I was on the ground, King Louie was a second farther away—a second closer to getting hit by a car or hurting someone. I had never considered the trails to be a dangerous place until that moment.

Suddenly Mom was bending down beside me. In all my life, I had never been so happy to see her. She gathered me up and put me in the car that was waiting on the road next to the trail.

I found out later that, while I thought I was out alone on the trails, so mature in the big wide world, Mom had been quietly following me in her car. She would stay just far enough back that I would not notice her presence.

When she scooped me up that day, I knew that, even when I did not think I needed her, she had my back.

When the doctor asked Mom to lie down on the couch so he could check her abdomen, her face paled, and she hesitated. Her eyes flitted to me in panic, and I nodded with encouragement. "It's okay, Mom," I said.

She accepted the doctor's hand, and he supported her as she lowered onto her back.

He lifted her shirt and there it was. Her respirations increased and her chest moved up and down rapidly. She could not hide her shortness of breath any longer.

"Oh," the doctor said.

My heart rose. Was this enough to make him understand that we needed their help?

She coughed as the doctor helped her up, and then smiled with a little embarrassment. I was not sure why, but whatever it was, that half-embarrassed smile made me want to cry.

I fought the familiar constricting in my chest as the doctor spoke.

"Yes," he said, "She's a good candidate for hospice."

The air grew silent. I reached back for the rocking chair arm and lowered myself into the seat as relief and dread struck me simultaneously—relief that they were here to help and dread that needing them, *truly needing* them, was confirmation that the end of our time with Mom was drawing near.

As the doctor finished his talk, he reminded Mom that it was possible to graduate from hospice. There was a softness in his eyes, in all their eyes. And I knew these people would help us take another step along the bridge.

Chapter 16: Bring the Outdoors In

Mid-June

*A*s she increasingly struggled to breathe, it was clear that Mom could no longer venture outside. There would be no more rolling her wheelchair into the yard, no more smelling the fresh air. It was another definitive step along the bridge, one that saddened me, and yet I felt I could not bring up the elephant in the room—that Mom was never going to get better.

"I don't want to make your mom upset," Dad said on multiple occasions to explain why we should absolutely, under no circumstances, talk about the fact that she was dying.

And I did not want to make her upset either. But with each step away from normalcy, I wondered how much longer we could *not* talk about it.

I contained my thoughts until hospice offered to provide us with a spiritual leader. They explained that she would talk to Mom about her beliefs and feelings, and then try to create an environment that reflected them.

The woman who showed up at our door was of average height, with pale skin and long red hair. Her features were plain, but her presence was pure comfort. She, of course, introduced herself when she arrived, but her name never stuck; I always called her what she was for us, "The Spiritual Leader."

She sat and talked with Mom, asking her questions about her upbringing in the Southwest and the Indian pottery displayed around my parents' house. And eventually, she left a space open to talk about the current situation.

"I would like to talk about what's happening to me," Mom said in a quiet voice. Her eyes shifted beyond the den. "I'm not sure others want me to, though."

Relief washed over me in the comfort of The Spiritual Leader's presence. Mom *did* want to talk about it, just like I did.

"Well, do you know what the American Indians do?" The Spiritual Leader asked.

She revealed that she had taken lessons from them and had learned that the men and women created separate sweat lodges, safe spaces where they could have private time away from each other to talk freely. In their tradition, we would make the den, the place Mom spent most of her time, into a sweat lodge. She loved the idea the instant we presented it to her.

We sprinkled Mom's collection of Indian pottery around the room and played American Indian music that Dad had found online. The den was transformed before our eyes into a space for spiritual rejuvenation.

The Spiritual Leader asked Mom to pick one of the clay pots that had a lid. Mom pointed to a circular one about three inches tall, sporting a masked bird with turquoise earrings painted on its center. The colors were beautiful: black, beige, brown, and rust blended perfectly across the image.

While Mom rested, The Spiritual Leader and I went into the yard and collected pieces of nature. As I stepped outside, I remembered a time when Mom had done something like this for me, thirty years earlier.

It was a beautiful spring afternoon, and high school had let out for the day. A few friends and I decided to venture to our local Family Fun Center. The bright colors and flashing lights drew us to the "Fun Zone." There were arcade games and miniature golf, but the most enticing activity was the gigantic, circular trampoline. It was as tall as I was high and three times my height in width. It had netting around its perimeter to stop us from flying off—perfectly safe for our rambunctious group. We jumped and flipped, joked and laughed . . . until I bounced just a little too high and was thrown off the trampoline and into the support springs.

I thought I heard a snap. A twinge of pain shot through my lower back.

Still laughing, I tried to move. But to my dismay, I was not only hurt, but also stuck. Everyone else got off the trampoline, and when I did not, they finally realized something was wrong. The laughing stopped. My friends tried to pull me out, but my leg was twisted like a pretzel under the trampoline. They called the workers over to help, and they gently untangled me from the springs. I rolled onto the trampoline, like a seal on land. Though I could move all parts of my body, moving my legs caused a sharp pain along my spine, like a knife twisted into my back. Fear began to overtake the pain as I lay there, waiting for rescue.

Mom was called.

A swift trip to the ER, many X-rays, and four hours later, Mom and I heard the diagnosis. There was no damage to my spine, but the ligaments around the right lumbar side of my back were injured. The doctor was firm. Healing meant one thing:

"You are going to need to stay in bed. For at least six weeks."

On the way home my mind raced. I was tired, and the pain in my back was growing. I worried about school. I worried about not seeing my friends, not seeing the outdoors for six weeks. I worried about being stuck in bed.

"Don't worry. We will make a plan," my mom said calmly, firmly.

That night she came to my bedside and wiped away my tears. "First thing tomorrow, I'm going to your school to talk with your counselor and figure out how you can do all your schoolwork from home."

I nodded.

"Next we're going to reorganize your room so that everything you need will be in reach of your bed," she said.

I drifted off to sleep, Mom watching me. In just under a day, her role had expanded into caregiver, teacher, friend, and therapist.

For the next six weeks, Mom altered her schedule and transformed my room into a workable recovery center. I had a place to do my homework, a medication schedule, a television, and new records. Mom brought a phone to my bedside so I could chat with friends in the evenings. She kept my room picked up and my side table stocked with everything I needed. The weeks went by in a blur, and instead of being alone and depressed, I was surrounded with activity and support.

Now, thirty years later, I was bringing the outdoors in for Mom.

The Spiritual Leader and I walked around the yard, gathering rocks, pinecones, weathered bark, and flowers. I felt myself awakening, becoming acutely aware of the nature surrounding me. This serenity outside of daily living was so much bigger than me and Mom and these rules we had been living by. The wind still whistled in our pain, the trees still swayed to its rhythm, the flowers still grew below the sun that still rose. As I collected pieces of nature, I reveled in them, outside of time and space, completely free. The rocks and twigs and pinecones, they were so much more than that. They were love and freedom and beauty, boundless messages within which I could envelop Mom and this awful time.

We entered the sweat lodge, which now felt more like a sanctuary, and released the items into the clay pot. The Spiritual Leader placed the lid back on top, and set it on the table in the center of the room.

The three of us sat in a small circle as The Spiritual Leader explained how the pot would be used. Whenever we wanted to talk, the lid of the pot would be removed. When we were done, the lid would be replaced. Along with the new rules for our spiritual setting, she helped us create a healing mental barrier within this sacred space.

I knew in that moment that I would not be able to nurse Mom back to health. But I could nurse her spirit. And mine.

I took the lid off and said, "Mom, remember the time I fell off the trampoline?

Chapter 17: Let Go of Anger

Late June

I opened the door for The Spiritual Leader, who stood still in its threshold, eyes wide.

"Do you see this?" she asked.

A small movement to the right of her head stole my attention. A red dragonfly, beating its wings at lightning speed, was hovering like a helicopter just over her shoulder.

I looked into its perfectly round, ant-like, brown eyes peering straight at me.

The Spiritual Leader said matter-of-factly, "You need to let go of any anger you have."

Her words struck me. "Really? I don't think I'm angry," I said.

But the red dragonfly did not move.

Again she spoke. "The dragonfly is here to give you this message. So just remember to let go of your anger, now or whenever you feel it. And in the future, if you see a red dragonfly, take it as a sign."

Then, as if on cue, this red dragonfly zoomed away into the yard.

The Spiritual Leader walked inside as if nothing happened.

But to me, seeing the red dragonfly was an extraordinary event. I was in awe, but also confused. I did not feel angry. Yet as I stood in the hallway, I realized what I did feel was numb. So entrenched was I in the daily routine of taking care of Mom that I did not allow myself to register my emotions. Survival mode was a way of life. My father's words of wisdom from so many years ago were etched in my mind: I was a Cornell. I was tough. I could take it.

That afternoon, I heard the hum of a car engine cut out. Mom had just fallen asleep. I crept to the front door and peered through the peephole. My sister and her boys were approaching from the driveway. I opened the door slowly to alleviate the moan of the metal hinges that could wake Mom up.

"Mom had a hard morning," I whispered as my sister pushed through the door. "Can we be quiet? She just got to sleep."

My sister barely glanced at me as she ushered her boys toward Mom's bedroom. "Come on boys. You can go see your Nana," she said at normal volume.

I stood alone in the open doorway, my jaw set as the sound of creaking bedsprings and laughter reached my ears. *Had she even heard me?* The fire in my gut ignited as I thought of how standoffish my sister had become toward me in the past few months. But as my nephews' laughter grew, a thought occurred to me. That maybe she resented me for being there more than she could. That she was just as angry with me for telling her not to bother Mom as I was that she had not listened. I took a deep breath and quelled the fire in my gut.

With Mom sleeping more and more of the day and night, there was not much communication between my dad, my sister, and me. We were all living our separate lives, held together by the fine thread of Mom barely living—a thread that was weakening with each passing day.

That evening, Dad ambled into the kitchen as I set the spaghetti sauce to simmer on the stove.

"How was your day?" I asked.

"Good," was all he said.

As he relinquished his wallet and keys to the counter, I wondered if he realized everything I had been doing for their household. Giving Mom her medicine, doing the laundry, de-cluttering their home, grocery shopping, making dinner, doing the dishes . . . all so Dad did not have to deal with anything except tending to Mom when he got home. And yet, I knew Mom did not want Dad to watch her dwindle away, and I knew he could not face her dying. That he lay awake all night beside Mom, listening for the subtlest indication that she had stopped breathing. That he slept fitfully, knowing any of those breaths taken between dreams could be her last.

As I walked down the driveway to my car, I scanned the yard for the red dragonfly. It was nowhere to be found. Hidden once again in the landscape, waiting for another moment to deliver its message—a reminder of emotions lurking just beneath the surface, a signal to acknowledge them and let them out.

Chapter 18: Don't Miss the Small Stuff

Early July

*T*he fresh air diffused the overpowering smell of polish and lotions as my aunt wheeled Mom through the open front door of the familiar peach-colored beauty salon. Water was already filling in the bowls of two of the four pedicure spa chair stations. A third tub of water rested beside one of the manicure tables, chair absent. My aunt maneuvered Mom's wheelchair beside the manicure station and Mom smiled at the kind women who had been doing her nails for years. Their returned smiles thinly veiled a palpable sadness.

As they set us up at our stations, I noticed Mom looking to the far wall where a large mirror hung. It was just higher than eye level. She stretched her neck, like a baby bird reaching for its mother's open beak.

I shook my head, amused, and glanced to my aunt who giggled. We had purposely avoided mirrors, not wanting

Mom to worry about her dwindling appearance. And yet here she was, trying desperately to answer the one question she always asked herself:

Do I look okay?

But the salon workers, single-minded in their mission, paid no attention. They hustled around, preparing, grabbing materials, adding in bath salts, checking the temperature of the water.

It was clear these women wanted to give Mom the small gift of comfort, of being pampered—if only for a few minutes.

I looked down at Mom's toenails as the pedicurist put away the nail clippers. They were still so long.

"Could you cut her nails shorter?" I asked.

The woman lifted Mom's foot so I could see her toenails better. "I can't make them shorter."

I squinted down at them. They were oblong ovals with no excess white nail at the end. As the woman said, they were cut as short as they could be.

Several realizations hit me at once. That I did not know what my own mother's toenails looked like, that I had only ever seen Mom's nails covered with polish, that this was the first time Mom and I had gotten our nails done together—even though it was a regular part of our respective lives—and that I did not even know that I *wanted* to know what Mom's nails looked like, but now that I did I wanted to know more.

A heavy weight settled on my chest.

What else was there to learn about her before I lost the chance?

Chapter 19: Be Grateful for Each Day

Early July

O ne evening after Mom had taken her medication, I stayed while she prepared for bed. Heavily medicated, Mom was clearly in a fog. She hunched on her make-up chair just in front of her bathroom sink. Slowly, with effort, she picked up her toothbrush. She dragged her arm back and forth in an attempt to brush her teeth.

What was such a simple action for most of us was now a phenomenal chore for Mom.

I wanted to help, and yet I did not want to take away her dignity in that moment. I could see she was proud that she could still care for herself.

After about fifteen minutes, Dad entered and noticed that she was struggling to finish the chore. He gently pried the toothbrush from her hand and rinsed it off. He offered her a little glass of water.

Dad turned on the shower, which was now equipped with a chair so she could sit while he washed her and shaved her legs.

As he gingerly guided her into it, I said my goodbyes for the night.

Then I made my way to my car.

Numbness transformed into homesickness.

So much was changing. I was losing my mom. But I also could not shake the undeniable feeling that I was losing my whole family. Time and illness were bleeding into our lives, drowning the joy, and carrying us further and further apart. This was not how it was supposed to happen.

Tears sobbed out of me in waves as I drove home. The roads were oddly clear of traffic, the sun dimming in the sky. I felt utterly alone in the world. Helpless that there was nothing I could do to save my mom. Angry that I was helpless. Too sad to be angry. Too exhausted to be sad.

The sky surrounded my car the whole way home, awash in a display of fiery orange and red, then softened by wisps of cloudless pink ribbons. I drove and cried and watched it changing—this uncontrollable, beautiful thing.

And in the stillness of the beauty, I was surprised by an overriding thought:

I am so grateful to have had another day with Mom.

Chapter 20: Create a Family Symbol

Mid-July

 My parents' front door opened before I could insert my key into the lock. Dad appeared on the other side of the threshold.

"In a hurry for Donut Tuesday?" I asked, referring to the meeting he and his friends held on Tuesday mornings.

His face was pale, the bags beneath his eyes darker than usual. "Your mom had a hard night. I called your aunt over."

"Is everything okay?" I asked in a whisper, peering toward the open bedroom door.

"She's getting worse," he said. "Last night lying next to her, I couldn't tell if she was breathing. I'm worried . . ." He pressed his lips together and looked away.

I swallowed the lump in my throat and took his hand. The truth had been staring us in the face for weeks. The pace of the disease was increasing, taking Mom down faster and harder. The end was most likely weeks away. And we didn't have a burial plan. Or any plans past taking care of Mom.

When my aunt arrived, Dad and I snuck out of the house and drove to the only place we could think of—the small, quiet cemetery a mile down the hill from Mom and Dad's house. It was nestled in the bottom edge of the slope, surrounded by some of the same hills as their home.

My body felt heavy as we drove around the winding cemetery road in silence. Beside the lush hills and clear sky, Dad appeared faded—his blue eyes almost gray, his gray hair whiter, his skin pale. As if the cowboy in him had dwindled away.

"It's beautiful, isn't it?" I finally said, voice low.

Dad nodded, and further down the road, he pointed across me. "There—that spot over there, near the back corner."

I craned my neck to see a particularly green and shady area.

"She would still see the sun coming up over the hills," he said.

It was indeed the same view they had gazed upon from their home for the last thirty-five years.

At the entry to the cemetery office stood two men, tall and gaunt, dressed in black suits. Their somber affect and the dull office décor behind them starkly contrasted with the natural beauty of the surrounding land.

A wave of sadness came over me as they greeted us. No smiles, no condolences. No family pictures in their office, no flowers adding a splash of color to the white walls or metal furniture. It was as if the place itself were dead, which made the trip that much harder.

Dad asked the taller of the two men about the partic- ular spot he had found for Mom.

The man examined the cemetery map—the only semblance of "artwork" on the walls. It was covered with numbers corresponding to plots, but no indication of which were vacant. Without turning around he said, "Yes, that area is available."

He drove us out on a golf cart to the spot near the back corner. We all took in the beauty, the silence, the serenity. It was perfect for Mom, but when I looked down, my feet were covering a name on a plaque. I jerked backward and spun to find another plaque, just a couple feet away. On one side of the open plot were more plaques, arranged like a checkerboard. I shivered at their closeness.

"She'll be surrounded by strangers," I said quietly.

Dad took my hand. "What if we make this a plot for the whole family, for the Cobblers?" Dad asked.

A small laugh found its way out of me. "Well then, we would have a Cobbler Clump."

It was summertime and raining in the Pacific Northwest. Our entire family, Mom and Dad included, had taken a weeklong vacation ending in Seattle. It had started as a business trip for my dad, but my sister and brother-in-law had recently moved back into town after ten years away, and with my young girls, who were six and eight, it was undeniable that our family dynamics were different. At home, in real life, we couldn't seem to find the time to get together as a family, so this trip was an attempt to reconnect. I bundled my California girls in tourist sweatshirts and plastic ponchos, and around we all wandered with umbrellas in hand.

Our first night in town, a local directed us to a hole-in-the-wall restaurant. The tension was palpable in the air as we sat down at the table. My girls, usually well-mannered at meals, were soggy and antsy after a long day of sightseeing in the rain. My sister and I couldn't seem to find common ground to converse. And Mom's eyes bulged as she watched us devour the bread and butter before we had even ordered.

When the waitress came by and asked if we wanted dessert, all of us looked to Dad.

"We'll have the cobbler," he said, patting Mom's hand. How could she deny her husband his favorite dessert?

Deep bowls arrived, filled with juicy, local blueberries, hot and sweet, covered with a delectable crust that was crisp and crumbly, but melted in our mouths. And, of course, it was all topped off with a large scoop of vanilla bean ice cream that mingled with the dough. We ate every single bite.

There was no doubt about it. We had become obsessed.

Though we ventured to other restaurants for the freshly caught seafood, we hustled back to the hole-in-the-wall for cobbler. After a few nights, we ordered it to go so we could sneak it back to the hotel room and gobble it up in our pajamas.

One night while we sat waiting for the cobbler, a hostess walked up to us and asked if we were the Smith family. Without missing a beat Dad said, "No, we're the Cobblers." And that was it. From that moment on, whenever our entire family got together, we were officially the Cobblers heading out on "a cobbler run." As the Cobblers, we were whole.

The morning after visiting the cemetery with Dad, I walked into their house to find him and Mom at the dining room table, eyes teary.

"I told her about our plot," Dad said.

The word "our" hung in the air. The underlying message was that, one day, we would all be together again.

I walked to the table and sat in the chair next to Mom. I took her hand in mine and kissed it.

All she said was, "I cannot believe it."

Chapter 21: Listen to the Bells Ring

Mid-July

*T*he clinking of the red table bell allowed Mom to still have a voice.

Now bedridden, she could no longer visit in the den, the kitchen, or even make it to the bathroom. Her bed, and the few feet that surrounded it, became her entire world. On her dresser lay the TV and a host of items she would never use again. Weakness was claiming her.

Around the bed we scattered the two rocking chairs from the living room and a couch from the den so that family and friends could visit in comfort. Mom watched and listened to the sounds of life going on around her. She began observing more, participating less.

She was almost done crossing the bridge.

But she could still look out the bedroom window at the rolling hills that gently sloped until they met a white picket fence.

And she could still ring that little red bell.

Mom loved the bell, maybe a little too much.

She rang it if she needed some water.

She rang it if she needed a tissue.

She rang it if she needed to say hello, or if she hadn't heard from us in a while.

She rang it, and we came running.

One time, she rang the bell and I hustled from across the house, just to find her there—smiling.

She didn't need anything in particular. There were no words between us, nothing to say. But she rang the bell and I came running, as if she had called me to be a witness that she was, indeed, still there.

In my neighborhood, church bells rang out every day. But for nearly twenty-five years, I never noticed them—not until Mom got her bell.

Suddenly, it was as if my ears had been tuned like a fine instrument to the rolling echo of one chime blending into the next. Sitting in my kitchen, I opened the window and let the melody permeate the room. Walking through town, I basked in the resonating tones, drawn toward them. Wherever I went, the bells brought me to a place of serenity. Because in the noise was the reminder that Mom was still, and always would be, a part of the whole, a part of the air we all breathed.

Chapter 22: Always Celebrate

Mid-July

As I took down Mom's crystal flutes from the cabinet, the rumble of car engines grew louder, and then ceased. Our guests were early, their arrival sneaking up on me like Mom's progressing illness.

Her days were getting shorter. She had been sleeping more and more. She could no longer get out of bed, let alone move around. Her appetite was almost nonexistent, her energy waning, and her mind in a morphine fog.

My dad, sister, and I had been going through the motions of life like zombies. Our level of communication had been condensed to the bare minimum necessary to keep the household in check and Mom comfortable. Losing Mom was beginning to define our relationship.

Our family was operating in a raincloud of sadness, one that swelled and sagged a little further with each day.

Yet today, we were reaching for something different. Mom and Dad's fiftieth wedding anniversary was just under two weeks away and we decided that, despite the current situation, we would celebrate.

I popped my head into her darkened bedroom while my sister ran to answer the door. Mom looked exhausted. Dad had carefully propped her into a sitting position against the pillows, and I could see the traces of a smile on her lips. Dad returned the smile as he helped her pull on a cute sweat jacket. She sat up just a bit straighter as the hellos of her best friends carried in through the hall.

I slipped past the others to the kitchen and lined up the flutes on a tray. I poured the champagne into each glass, careful to make sure that the bubbles reached the top, but did not spill over. It occurred to me that this would be one of the most meaningful glasses of champagne I would ever share.

I placed a straw into Mom's flute, which would allow her to sip without choking. I took a deep breath and lifted the tray, walking gingerly into the bedroom.

Mom's eyes widened with excitement as I walked through the door. The group had created a loving circle around her. Dad stood proudly at her side. As I handed out the champagne, he shook his head, saying, "I can't believe we've been married fifty years." And then there it was— Mom flashed that smile that could light up any room.

When I was six years old, my family moved into our first house, in a neighborhood full of kids. Up until that point in my life, my only social interactions had been in the inviting classroom of kindergarten and with my baby sister, who was not yet a lively playing companion. I was used to entertaining myself in our old, childless neighborhood. And now, suddenly, I was the new kid on the block with no idea how to make friends.

For a week I stood looking out the family room window at the neighborhood kids, laughing and playing outside. Questions built up in my head. How would I say hello? Would I fit in? Would they want to play with me?

Mom busily unpacked boxes, getting the house in order, all the while watching me with curiosity and concern.

"Go, Lannette!" Mom said one day as she held my baby sister. "Go out and play, make some new friends."

But my feet would not move. No matter how lonely I felt, no matter how much I wanted to join in on the games, I just could not find the courage.

Mom sat down at the kitchen table with me. Smiled that big smile of hers. "What are you doing this Saturday?"

I shrugged my shoulders. Saturday was five days away, a lifetime for a six year old.

"Ever been to a backyard fair?" she asked.

I raised an eyebrow, and then shook my head no.

She took my hand and led me to our new backyard. I just could not see it. *What did she mean?*

"How do we make it a fair?" I wondered aloud.

"Just you watch," she said. And she went to work, making me her fearless assistant.

We began our preparations by creating invitations. We hand-drew colorful flyers with markers.

The next day we drove to the party store where she purchased bright decorations, tickets, and prizes.

We spent the third day decorating the backyard. We got cardboard and paint, and made all kinds of carnival games: throw the beanbags to knock down the bowling pins, throw the ping pong ball into the fish bowl full of water, toss the bean bag in the clown's mouth. We paid special attention to the log cabin playhouse that had been in our backyard when we moved in. No one had lived in the house before us, so my parents must have bought it for my sister and me, but to my six-year-old self it was just miraculously there. It had an A-frame roof that allowed me to stand inside it and still have room above my head, and a Dutch door. We kept the top half of the door open to act as a ticket booth and snack stand.

On the fourth day, Mom and I walked around the neighborhood with my little sister in her stroller. We introduced ourselves to the neighbors and handed out the invitations. I held my breath and waited for their reactions. Would they think the fair was stupid? Already be busy? Not want to play with me? But to my surprise, they all seemed excited to attend.

Saturday morning, Mom and I sifted through a box of my old dance costumes until we found the perfect one.

Soon after, I emerged from my new room all dressed up like a magical genie, wearing emerald green baggy pants, a shimmery top, and a little green hat on my head with sheer fabric draped around my face.

As if in a trance, I walked outside to the backyard. But it wasn't the backyard anymore. It was a dream-like fair. Parents talked and relaxed. The kids moved from one game to the next, collecting tickets when they won. I happily accepted the role of ticket master, sitting on the inside of the playhouse's Dutch door and exchanging winning tickets for prizes. From that day on, I knew everyone and they all knew me.

Looking into my glass of champagne, I mused how Mom had taken that shy, scared girl sitting at the window and turned her into a magical genie, excitedly greeting new friends.

Dad lifted his glass. "To my beautiful wife of fifty years."

A lightness washed over all of us as a smile spread on her lips. She was, in that moment, lit from within.

They clinked glasses and we all shouted out, "To fifty years!"

Mom sucked her champagne down before anyone else touched the flutes to their lips. I could hardly suppress my delight. It was as if the sun had broken free from the clouds, warmth and light opening up the space, inviting joy into the least likely of places.

This room, just a day before heavy with fear and loss, was now a carnival of family, laughter, and love.

Chapter 23: Listen Without Distraction

Late July

Silence was settling over the house like soot leftover from a wildfire, seeping into every crack and crevice. My ears ached for the rhythmic pinging of the red bell that still remained on Mom's bedside table.

There had been a definite turn. She no longer got up to brush her teeth. Her little chair by the bathroom sink sat unused. It no longer mattered to her what outfit she was wearing or what her hair looked like.

Most of the day she was unmoving as the morphine coma enveloped her.

Quiet.

Still breathing.

One morning, after brushing Mom's hair, I sat next to her. "All done, Mom," I said.

Her soft breath was barely audible above the room noise. Breathing was all she could respond with, all she could give now. And each day, each breath brought her closer to complete silence.

At first it was unnerving. Never again would we have a conversation. Never again would I hear her laugh. But as I sat with her and listened, her breath became her words.

And I cherished each one.

Chapter 24: Keep the Precious Moments Intimate

Late July

*M*om was now hovering between two worlds, no longer participating, no longer observing. My sister and I decided to spend the night at my parents' home—to hold onto each moment we had left. For a while, we had had months left with Mom . . . then weeks . . . then days . . . now we did not know. Could it be minutes?

As reality weighed on us, we had a choice. Sit and mope, or . . .

"Let's make a meal Mom loves, and eat it the three of us in the dining room." There was a sparkle in my sister's eyes as she said it—one that I had not seen in a while.

Of all Mom's favorite recipes, we knew the best one for this night—one that filled the house with savory goodness—Beef Bourguignon. My sister, Dad, and I flew into action, happy to have a mission that would connect us to Mom. Though none of us spoke the words, I sensed we all had the feeling this might be our last supper with her. We wanted to do her proud.

I'd prepared Beef Bourguignon before, but this time, this day was different. It was as if Mom's arms were guiding mine. Before we began cooking, we set the table in the dining room to the nines—a tablecloth, the best silver and china, napkins with holders, candles, and flowers—the way Mom would for a family holiday. All three of us moved in determined, solemn waves, locking eyes from time to time and choking back sadness.

I took a minute to check on Mom. The hallway light spilled into the darkness of the bedroom, the chopping and scraping in the kitchen undercutting the purring of the oxygen tank. Her silhouette lay nearly still on the bed. Through the dim light I could just make out the shallow rising and falling of her chest. I stood and breathed in sync with her, listening to my own breath, imagining it was hers.

As I moved back into the kitchen, my sister and I shared a meaningful glance:

Yes, I wish Mom were making us this meal too.

The wall that had been between us for years—the one that had been growing taller and thicker as Mom got worse—was no longer there. My sister's eyes reflected the same sadness and fear swirling in my heart. Since we had become adults, she hadn't let herself need me, hadn't let me in. But those eyes were the eyes of my baby sister. The one I'd rescued from careless babysitters, from the top of a bucket where a rattlesnake lay ready to pounce, from the hillside behind our house that she had accidentally rolled down. Yet now, at this moment, I was not the older sister.

We were a team, sharing strength to carry on in Mom's tradition.

We reminisced about how each birthday growing up, Mom gave us a choice of a homemade meal or going out to a restaurant. There was no contest. We both agreed: there was nothing better than one of Mom's home-cooked meals. And she knew it too.

She would carefully arrange all the ingredients and move with dexterity and precision from one station to the next. She was the master of her domain, organized, efficient—and the evidence was the heavenly smell of red wine, browned beef, and sautéed mushrooms.

All of us moved slowly and deliberately: I as I chopped the mushrooms, my sister as she cut the beef into cubes and then seasoned them with kosher salt and olive oil, Dad as he sliced the onions and carrots, and minced the garlic. Into the cast iron pot it all went. My sister poured in the heavy red wine. I added the fresh thyme and salted butter.

Past and present seemed to live as one. Everything we had been through together as a family was rising to the surface like the bubbles in the pot, the tension dissipating like the spiraling steam.

We spent many quiet minutes that night waiting for our beef stew to simmer, for all the ingredients to marry perfectly. The rich aroma was all around us, permeating down the hall, into the family room, the living room, the den, and—most importantly—Mom's room.

We huddled at one end of the dining room table with our decorations, our red wine, and our stew. Mom's presence was with us in the crystal stem glasses, the china bowls, and the hum of her oxygen tank from the other room. Comfort enveloped me as I took my first bite of the beef bourguignon, the complex, intertwining flavors melting in my mouth.

It had been so long since it was just the four of us, perhaps as far back as when I was seventeen. No husbands, no kids. Just our nuclear family gathered around a perfect meal. Not made by Mom, but, nonetheless, made with her presence.

The peace surrounding us that night will forever be embedded in my memory.

And it was, indeed, our last supper with Mom.

Chapter 25: It's Okay to Let Go

July 25th

The chime of the grandfather clock striking ten reverberated down the hall and into the bedroom. Mom lay still in bed as the hospice nurse assessed her. My sister and I stood at the end of the bed, arms crossed, jaws set.

The hospice nurse leaned down and whispered in Mom's ear, "Your family is here with you. It's okay to let go."

She signaled to me and slipped out of the room. I followed after her and walked her to the front door. She explained that Mom's body had begun the final process of shutting down. She told me that when the time came, I should place a note on the door letting visitors know that we needed some time alone to grieve. Then she took my hands, her eyes fixed on mine. "If there's anything you want to say to your mom, now's the time to say it."

Her words cut loose the emotional rubber band that had been stretching more and more tautly inside of me for weeks. For as long as I could remember, from the moment we got the diagnosis really, I had pushed myself into "caretaker" mode. As a nurse, this was a natural place for me to be. My role was as the support system, the strength, the source of unwavering faith and calm. I had vowed never to break down.

Yet Mom no longer needed my care. And truth be told, I needed the nurse's words to jolt me from my stoic caretaker stance. I needed permission to just be a daughter grieving the final moments of her mother's life.

Reality swirled around my head. This was happening, and happening *now*.

I shut the door behind the nurse, my eyes glancing over to my aunt who smiled wanly from the back patio. I rushed back into the bedroom. My sister glanced up at me as I knelt beside Mom.

I exploded into a whirlwind of despair, letting out a cry that had been stuck in my throat for the better part of a year. Tears flooded. My heart sank to a place I did not know it could go.

I took Mom's hand in mine, the words bursting out of me with uncontrollable force. "Mom, I know you know this, but I want to tell you again how much I love you. I will never forget you. I will remember you at the sight of every butterfly or when sipping a glass of champagne."

Though unable to respond, I felt that Mom had heard me.

My sister grasped my shoulder, her eyes glassy and voice shaky. "That was really beautiful," she said.

I stood up and grappled with my cell phone, called my husband and asked him to bring our girls to Mom's side so they could say their last goodbyes, then hung up the phone.

Dad, my sister, my aunt, and I sat solemnly in the now-sacred room.

The only sound was that of Mom breathing.

And each breath she took got softer.

And softer.

And then Mom started muttering unintelligible words. The hospice nurse had prepared us for this phenomenon, called "chattering." She had told us that it happens in almost all cases right before a person passes. We watched in awe as Mom smiled, giggled, and chattered for about five minutes.

As we witnessed this exchange, I could feel that something special, something sort of magnificent was happening. *Were we watching a conversation with those waiting for her on the other side? Would they be the ones who would help her travel from our existence to theirs?*

Dad was at her side holding her hand, checking her pulse. My sister, my aunt, and I were still standing at the edge of the bed.

It was the very end. And she was hovering.

"I love you, Mom." I said again.

"Her pulse quickened when you said that," Dad said. Then he asked us all for quiet.

Dad knew his wife. He wanted her to go in peace and not feel compelled to stay. Mom was powerful in that way, and we all knew that some part of her soul wanted to remain with us.

Her chattering continued and she seemed to be releasing, as if she knew it was okay to go, okay to follow those who were there to lead her.

Then in one forceful movement, her chest lifted up, pulling her head up after it. Her lips pursed and one last breath rattled out of her mouth. No inhaling, just a forced release of a long, strong, loud exhale.

Her body moved back to the bed, lying flat once more. Then—no more breath.

Mom had passed.

As we all looked on we noticed that the change was sudden, almost unbelievable.

Her face was instantly free of stress, free of wrinkles or worldly fear. She looked like a teenage girl. She was more beautiful than I had ever seen her.

Chapter 26: Memories in Dragonflies

*U*ntil my experience with Mom, dragonflies had not held any real significance. I never noticed how many drop in from time to time—in the park, in the garden, at the beach, on the street corner.

And now when I see one, it's like a gentle reminder, a small gift to open.

I stop. And I watch.

And allow time to stand still—just a little.

Blurred motion, darting from place to place. The wings a frenzied dance.

And in this stillness of time, I am instantly transported back to Mom and the entire process of her passing. When she was diagnosed, there was no question I would be by her side to the end. I was compelled the way we are compelled to eat, to breathe. And in that certainty, in that time I explored with Mom, a new spirituality was born within me.

The journey I took with her as she crossed the bridge taught me the absolute beauty of slowing down to the pace of a dying soul.

Colors became more vivid.

Listening was a way of being.

A sacred connection grew in that space between Mom and me, one I can feel even to this day.

So when I see a dragonfly now, I don't meet its presence with sadness, but with gratitude. For the gentle reminder it brings me.

To stop. And pay attention to whatever is happening right now. To pause and dive inside the moments we let fly by us in the blurry speed of modern life.

Because in an instant, that creature is gone.

Yet it always leaves me with the same message.

And it's the kind of message that can only be whispered in love between souls on opposite ends of the bridge.

Acknowledgments

I have been so blessed to be the mother of my two girls, Alesse and Melissa. While raising them, I was their muse, always trying to open them up to the possibilities, to show them ways they might pave their way in the world. Little did I know that they would do the same for me. Our relationship has become much more than the traditional mother–daughter one. They have become my best friends and my confidantes. I cannot thank them enough for all the support and love they have given me in life and through the ups and downs as I wrote this book. It has truly been a family affair. Alesse, always reading and rereading, adding thoughts and offering encouragement. Melissa, spending countless hours helping me write, rewrite, edit, and tell the story of love from her mom to her nana.

To my husband, Todd, who had no idea that a book would come out of watching me care for my mom through her illness. I thank him for being so unselfish, sharing me with my mom through her end and through all the hours of writing and rewriting my story so it could truly impart the feelings I had held so closely in my heart.

To my sister, Kendall, whom I love so dearly, and who went through this time in her own way. I cherish you and, yes, I wish Mom were still here too.

To my dad, for always standing by his family and for loving my mom.

To all my family, especially my aunt, Pat, and cousin, Kristle. For our lifetime of experiences together, with Mom and after. You are my special peeps. Thank you for the encouragement you offer daily.

To my mom's best friend, Darlene. You are a beautiful, positive person. Your energy helped my mom so much, and continues to help me. I know Mom is still laughing at your stories and jokes.

To Barbara Basia-Koenig, for the spiritual inspiration you give to me. You have enriched my life so.

After months of writing my story, my daughter Melissa took me to the La Jolla Writer's Conference. She recommended I take a class on memoir writing. In doing so, I introduced myself to the teacher, Marni Freedman. I explained I had written a story about my mom and it was done. She laughed, saying, "Are you open for structural change?"

"Yes, of course," I said.

She became my writing coach, pulling stories out of my memory and guiding me through many rewrites. What began as *Mom and Me* turned into *Memories in Dragonflies*.

Marni, I cannot thank you enough for all your expertise and for believing in me and my story.

To Jeniffer Thompson, for helping to bring my story out into the world and understanding what it was about: simple lessons, simple moments, simple joys through life.

Special thanks to my beta readers: Marlena Schmidt Fiol, PhD, Anastasia Hipkins, Tracy Jones, and Phyllis Olin for their indispensible insight and input.

To all hospice facilities and organizations, for being there so families can stay together through the end.

To Brooke Warner and She Writes Press, for making this book a reality.

About the Author

*L*annette Cornell Bloom is a registered nurse, speaker, and author. She is passionate about bringing simple joys to others. As an RN and health practitioner of more than thirty years, she has seen firsthand the need to care for others both emotionally and physically. She brings into focus the fragility of life and the importance of enjoying the simple joys that slip through our fingers if we're not paying attention—because life may be hard, but joy is simple. Lannette currently lives in La Jolla, California, with her husband and two pugs. Learn more at www.simplejoys.com.

Author photo © Alesse Bloom

Selected Titles from She Writes Press